"...Fashionable, Neat, and Good..."

The Williamsburg Collection of
Antique Furnishings

The Williamsburg Antique

"... let them be fashionable, neat, and good in their several kinds ..."

— GEORGE WASHINGTON,
ordering merchandise from his
London agent, April 15, 1757.

Collection of Furnishings

THE COLONIAL WILLIAMSBURG FOUNDATION
Williamsburg, Virginia

Distributed by Holt, Rinehart and Winston, Incorporated
New York, New York

Library of Congress Catalog Card Number 73-86811

Colonial Williamsburg ISBN   0-87935-018-0 (hardbound)
                              0-87935-017-2 (paperbound)

Holt, Rinehart and Winston ISBN   0-03-089462-X (hardbound only)

Printed in the United States of America

IN 1933, just before the opening of the Governor's Palace, Mr. John D. Rockefeller, Jr., wrote Mr. and Mrs. Harry Long of Cohasset, Massachusetts, who had donated an antique musical instrument to Colonial Williamsburg:

> It has long been our hope that what we have been doing in Williamsburg would ultimately and increasingly as time goes on stir the interest of people all over the country who possess colonial antiques. We have further hoped that many of these people would feel that restored Williamsburg offered the best permanent resting place for the appropriate and outstanding pieces in their collections. In this way we have envisioned the ultimate enrichment of the collection of antiques at Williamsburg until it should become second to no collection of its kind in the country.

For more than forty years, guided by these principles, Colonial Williamsburg has assembled its collection of early English and American furnishings with the goal of making it authentically appropriate to eighteenth-century Williamsburg as well as second to none in the United States.

Each year, many public-spirited donors have joined us in

this work. All the while, of course, our curators have been enlarging, changing, re-evaluating our collection. This thriving activity, one of growing complexity and importance, has occupied the time and energy of a remarkable staff.

We have made significant and exciting progress toward the goal Mr. Rockefeller set for Colonial Williamsburg. Some twenty years ago the magazine *Antiques* described the collection as "one of the outstanding collections in this country," and in 1969, when three additional eighteenth-century buildings were opened to the public, *Antiques* added: "The collection has grown to such an extent in both quantity and quality that to call it outstanding seems almost an understatement."

Today, it is fair to say, the collection of early English furnishings is the finest in the United States. The American collection, likewise, is one of the half-dozen best of its kind. Together, they comprise a unique assemblage, mingling as they do representative furnishings in both fields.

Unlike most museums, Colonial Williamsburg has never had an accessions committee. Until Mr. Rockefeller died, in 1960, he approved major additions to the collection in consultation with my predecessor, Mr. Kenneth Chorley. Mr. Rockefeller maintained his keen interest in this program. When an object was presented he considered its beauty and worth, then almost invariably asked, "Is this the kind of thing that would have been in Williamsburg?" Since 1960 I have personally approved new acquisitions on the recommendation of our curators. This has enabled us to move readily and efficiently in the building of the collection, without recourse to the committee system.

The Curators

Colonial Williamsburg has been fortunate in its small group of dedicated and talented curators who have built the collection from its beginnings in the 1920s. These remarkable people, with their staffs and advisers, have been responsible for assembling a collection whose hallmarks are quality and authenticity.

Thomas Jefferson owned a number of fine violins, including a Cremona. This beautiful violin was made by Tomasso Balestrieri in 1757.

Three names in particular are associated with the earliest days. The pioneers were William Graves Perry and Susan Higginson Nash of the Boston architectural firm of Perry, Shaw and Hepburn, which guided the development of the restoration of Williamsburg. Mr. Perry acquired the first furnishings and Mrs. Nash directed their use in the exhibition buildings. They received major assistance from Louis Guerineau Myers, who was then treasurer of the Rockefeller Foundation. This trio laid the foundations on which today's extensive collection is based.

In 1931 James L. Cogar began an eighteen-year career as the first official curator, and Colonial Williamsburg will always be indebted to him for the extensive and appropriate additions he made to the growing collection of antique furnishings. Mr. Cogar's dedication, taste, and perception resulted in contributions that were invaluable.

Mr. Cogar was succeeded in 1950 by John M. Graham II, who for twenty years expanded the scope and improved the quality of the collection in every way. His broad experience in the field of eighteenth-century furnishings enabled Mr. Graham to expand the collection on the soundest basis, and the great strengths of the collection are due in large measure to his knowledge and foresight. Mr. Graham's distinguished contribution pre-dated his official career here, in fact, for he actually was acquiring furnishings for Colonial Williamsburg before he became curator.

Since 1971, Colonial Williamsburg has been fortunate to have as its curator Graham Hood, an accomplished scholar and author. Mr. Hood is carrying on the tradition of high-caliber work in the field of the decorative arts in Williamsburg. The inspiring freshness of his point of view is already making itself felt in the natural, "lived-in" effects now achieved in many period rooms. He has assisted with this publication and his comments on hundreds of pieces from the collection follow later in these pages.

Though the building of Colonial Williamsburg's collections has been a major objective for more than forty years, we realize that the task can never be completed, since our goal is not merely to create a traditional museum. Ours is a working collection. There is nothing static about it. In effect, it circulates through the equivalent of more than 200 gallery rooms. Not even the surviving eighteenth-century buildings of Williamsburg are more important to our interpretation of colonial life than the 100,000 pieces we use to create life-like settings in the interiors of the homes, shops, taverns, and public buildings of the town.

Miss Alice Winchester, the distinguished former editor of *Antiques,* took note of this: "The antiques at Williamsburg are even more than an outstanding collection. In their present settings they have two virtues that are particularly impressive. One is that they are so thoroughly documented...the other impressive thing...is that their arrangement in the buildings is not only pleasing but convincing."

Obviously such a collection, used in the interpretation of social history, can never be too large or too complete. I realize that millions of people have taken home widely differing impressions of the quality and scope of our collection, and this, I think, is a tribute to its great variety, and to the skill with which our curators have put it to use. We are constantly trying to devise new ways to make these furnishings even more effective.

Thus, though these pages reveal the great range and depth of the collections of furniture, silver, ceramics, textiles, prints and paintings, and many other objects, it should be remembered that the work of the curators is never done. They will always play a leading role in Colonial Williamsburg's efforts to interpret the eventful past of this colonial capital.

Curatorial Storehouse

Much of their work is done behind the scenes, in the curator's offices and storage areas, where priceless and fragile objects are housed under carefully controlled conditions of temperature and humidity. Maintenance and repair, of course, require the constant attention of highly skilled specialists—for example, a gifted master cabinetmaker and an assistant devote full time to maintaining the furniture collection.

"A variety of toys, dressed and undressed babies" were advertised for sale at the Margaret Hunter Shop in the early 1770s. This doll is from our collection and was made around 1770.

Some of our friends, failing to understand the true function of our busy curatorial storehouse, which was the brainchild of John Graham, have thought of it as the home of surplus furnishings—and have concluded that Colonial Williamsburg has more objects than it can use. But these pieces are never stored and forgotten. They may go out tomorrow into a new setting in the Palace, or a tavern, or a kitchen, or to Carter's Grove plantation. Many will eventually appear in a museum of antique furnishings, of which I will say more later. In fact, our search for appropriate items is as keen—and as essential—as ever. In a time when such pieces are becoming increasingly rare, our need for representative Virginia pieces, for example, is as pressing today as it was forty years ago. And, as the interest of Americans in our past seems to intensify, the efforts of Colonial Williamsburg in this field seem to grow in significance.

The storage areas have another important function little known to the public—they house study collections which attract a stream of curators and scholars from the great museums of England and America. Seldom a week passes without a visit from one of these specialists, who see our collection in the storage area as well as in the exhibition buildings.

Growth of the Collection

Our growth in the field has been notable. In its first eight years Colonial Williamsburg furnished and exhibited three public buildings. In the following thirty years an additional forty-two shops, taverns, and houses have been furnished. Our collections have grown at a pace to match these developments. We hope to continue this effort.

Colonial Williamsburg, as an experiment in preservation, has always sought to make the past vivid and immediate to the modern public. Here our collections have been invaluable, for this has been attempted not simply through words or pictures but through the experience of a total environment, incorporating vir-

[5]

tually all the things that an inhabitant of that past time would have known.

The ideas and deeds of early Virginia leaders are much more fully realized when one can see the place in which they lived and worked, the ways they formed their lives, and the kinds of things they did from day to day. But an historical personage does not come to life simply because we learn of his part in battles or politics. It is more important that we visualize his social life, see his house inside and out, and gauge his intellectual pursuits and his amusements. This is the primary function of our furnishings. It would be quite accurate, however, to say that the collection itself is really a by-product of our effort to furnish the more than two hundred exhibition rooms, shops, and kitchens.

In forming the collection three principles have been observed.

Authenticity has been the paramount consideration, as is the case with all great museums. Fine reproductions have been used only when an antique has been judged unobtainable or, as in the case of some textiles, too fragile.

Of equal importance has been whether or not the objects were appropriate for eighteenth-century Williamsburg. The search for appropriate examples has resulted in a collection of almost unprecedented variety, for we must span a whole society, ranging from British royal governors and wealthy landowners to indentured servants and slaves. Our curators have found it necessary to seek, acquire, and display every conceivable type of household object because in effect we are furnishing an entire town.

Thirdly, there has always been the intent to collect related material for wider educational purposes. To understand the kind of furniture that a governor might have had, for example, and, by implication, to sense his social role, we have examined the general range of English and American furniture of the period, and acquired selected items that may not bear directly on Williamsburg. Through this broader approach our collections provide an insight into the whole English-speaking Atlantic community in the colonial period.

Judging whether a cup, chest, or coverlet is appropriate for

Made in Glasgow about 1760 by John Jeffray, this clock was owned by Lord Dunmore, the last royal governor of Virginia. It was in the Governor's Palace until 1776, when it was sold at auction. The clock was returned in 1965 as a gift in memory of Mr. and Mrs. Harrison Trent Nicholas of Lynchburg, Virginia.

eighteenth-century Williamsburg is not simply a matter of guess-work or intuition, although at times we must fall back on the latter. We have few complete objects for comparative purposes that we are absolutely sure were here in the colonial period; thus we have had to rely on the fruits of tireless and scrupulous research. Documentary evidence tells a great deal about what people bought, how much they bought (or sold), what they owned when they died, and what they thought precious enough to leave as heirlooms. Fortunately, we have inventories of the personal estates of many eighteenth-century Williamsburg residents—including those of Lord Botetourt, who died in 1770; Peyton Randolph, the first president of the Continental Congress, 1776; and Henry Wetherburn, tavern-keeper, 1760, to name only a few. These give a good picture of the type of furniture in their homes at the time of their deaths. The residences of these men are now open to the public as exhibition buildings and the inventories are used as guides to the interior furnishings.

These inventories are supplemented by other documentary information—letterbooks, account books, and wills—as well as by archaeological findings. An inventory may list simply so much "china," but our archaeological excavations have been most fruitful in revealing whether it was soft- or hard-paste porcelain, delft, or creamware, and exactly how it was decorated.

If Colonial Williamsburg were a typical museum the entire collection would be housed in an enormous building with scores of period rooms and galleries. However, as our task is to present an authentic picture of life in our eighteenth-century city, our galleries are widely scattered throughout the town and it is impossible for the visitor to see the total collection at once. This book attempts to review the collection as a whole and is the first in a series of published works designed to acquaint the public with our holdings.

The Period Room

Since the restoration of the city has required the creation of so many different interior settings throughout the Historic Area, the curators have furnished period rooms in almost unparalleled number and kind.

The period room, in fact, may well be the most imposing aspect of Colonial Williamsburg's program in this field, for in more than two hundred rooms the visual arts and historical research merge, and the collection meets its public. The period room as it is developed here departs from tradition—for this setting is as likely to be a tavern hall, a kitchen, a shop, or a craftsman's bedroom as a formal parlor or dining room. We are attempting the fullest possible interpretation of the city's eighteenth-century social life.

Through imaginative presentation by curators the period room can be as informative as a book, as visually appealing as a painting, and as evocative as a scene from a play. In fact, the successful period room has as much intellectual and spiritual import as an English group portrait or "conversation piece" of the eighteenth century. In this effort we have been most fortunate in locating extraordinary items, such as the billiard tables listed in tavern inventories, silver chamber pots, and even a fire engine of eighteenth-century style. The response of visitors to an appropriately arranged room that colonial Virginians seem to have left but a moment earlier is one of the most rewarding experiences to those of us who work here.

Like the furnishings themselves, these rooms are based on evidence, on contemporary inventories to determine *what* was used there, and on paintings and prints to illustrate *how* it was used. It is here, in these rooms, that the exceptional variety of the collection becomes so important. The English furniture collection, ranging from the most elaborate and sophisticated to the plainest and most provincial, is particularly strong in mid-eighteenth century pieces. American furniture is represented not only by an excellent New England group; there are also imposing groups by Pennsylvanian and other cabinetmakers of the middle colonies, and choice southern pieces as well. Fortunately, Virginia pieces in growing number are being acquired.

Among the most significant pieces on display are those with an eighteenth-century Williamsburg history, notably the handsome Speaker's chair of the House of Burgesses, on permanent loan from the commonwealth of Virginia. There are also several secretary desks and clothes presses that were here in colonial days—and we are making frequent additions, often through the generous cooperation of owners who, as Mr. Rockefeller foresaw, seek a safe and appropriate repository for their priceless heirlooms.

In the field of metalwork, seventeenth- and eighteenth-century royal silver is well represented, but there are many other pieces of outstanding beauty, some of the finest specimens of the silversmith's art—most of them needed to match inventories calling for elaborate table settings. Lord Botetourt not only owned a silver tureen and several silver sconces, but he also had thirteen dozen silver spoons of various sizes, sixty plates, twenty-seven dishes, and silver gilt-handled dessert knives in 1770. Among the items for which we are still searching is a massive silver tea kettle weighing over one hundred and thirty ounces, such as the one listed in Wetherburn's inventory of 1760. We have no idea how this tavern-keeper acquired such an imposing kettle, but its presence here is one more bit of evidence that furnishings of sophisticated taste were in daily use in eighteenth-century Williamsburg.

Among the rarities of the collection is a mid-eighteenth century mace that was used on ceremonial occasions by officials of the city of Williamsburg—including a celebration of the Treaty of Paris in 1783. We also have several pieces of silver made by James Geddy, recovered on the Geddy House and Palace sites by archaeologists. Furthermore, several pieces of Randolph family silver have been returned to the house they graced in the eighteenth century—examples of the type of singularly appropriate objects we are constantly seeking.

There is a great variety of good English pewter, brass, and copper and a large number of iron items—kitchen utensils by the score, fireplace equipment, and many other domestic forms—objects that are essential in the interpretation of daily life of the colonial era. For example, a small sharkskin box containing a set of a dozen silver cockspurs, only recently acquired, conjures up a graphic picture of one of colonial Virginia's most popular—if

Painted black, this iron warming machine or stove was made by Buzaglo in London by order of Lord Botetourt for use in the Capitol. A picture of Liberty with her hand resting on the Magna Carta and the Virginia Coat of Arms stand out in relief on the sides.

[9]

bloodthirsty—sports, once enjoyed by thousands of Virginians, including George Washington.

Archaeology, in combination with traditional historical research, has helped to document our collection of ceramics and glass. The work of Ivor Noël Hume and his staff has unearthed hundreds of thousands of fragments of eighteenth-century ware. It is significant that the excavation of the John Custis well revealed numerous broken wine glasses rarer than any in our collection. In his long and productive excavations of Williamsburg sites, Mr. Noël Hume has provided evidence that some of the city's eighteenth-century householders ate from fine porcelain and drank from the most handsome of glasses. Once sherds of such wares have been unearthed, our curators seek to acquire similar examples and place them in the exhibition buildings.

But documentary evidence alone told us that there were twenty-two "Chelsea China figures" in the Palace in 1770, half of them in the front parlor and half in the dining room. Many other such groups, of course, are mentioned in wills and inventories.

I have no hesitation in saying that the collections of Chelsea porcelain, English delft and Staffordshire slip-decorated pottery, enameled salt-glazed stoneware, and Wedgwood-Whieldon wares are unsurpassed. This was largely the work of John Graham, who made this field his specialty. The purchase of the truly outstanding Kauffman and Kidd collections of Chelsea porcelains and English pottery were of first importance. In addition to our purchases, many donors have aided in building this superb collection.

Eighteenth-century textiles, whose survival seems a miracle to many visitors, are essential as well as beautiful touches in almost every exhibition room. Cloth came into colonial Virginia in vast quantities, bearing names as colorful as the materials themselves—fustians, calamancoes, hollands, nankeens, russets, tiffinies, harrateens. Such textiles were used for clothing and window curtains, for dressing beds and tables, for upholstering furniture, even for covering floors.

In dress and furnishing silks of the late seventeenth and eighteenth centuries, brocaded silks, English printed textiles, and the myriad examples of needlework that eighteenth-century

Made in the period 1710-30, this English pedestal-stemmed wine glass, thrown into the John Custis well about 1759, was retrieved during an archaeological excavation in 1964.

women painstakingly completed, our collection is especially rich.

There is also a fine group of English and Oriental carpets and a representative number of women's gowns and men's suits, replete with countless accessories, shoes, purses, hats, and buckles dating from about 1725 to 1790.

Magnificent gifts have greatly augmented this collection in the last few years. To an already distinguished group of textiles (from which the Victoria and Albert Museum had borrowed for an exhibition) an anonymous donor added hundreds of examples, including costumes, beadwork, printed handkerchiefs, and a very large sampling of needlework. More recently Mrs. Francis H. Lenygon gave more than five hundred textile items, an important and valuable contribution that recalled the work of her husband in the 1930s as consultant to Mr. Rockefeller on antique furnishings. The result is one of the world's great assemblages of antique textiles.

Because of the inherent fragility of textiles, they are changed in the exhibition buildings twice a year—a small part of our program of conservation. Like other objects, they must also be cleaned, photographed, catalogued, and prepared for their next appearance on exhibition. This is another example of our need for well-equipped storerooms for proper maintenance of objects; but though the storeroom is a colorful room of infinite patterns, textures, and hues, it is only a temporary home for many of these textiles, which go back and forth to the exhibition buildings.

Historic Portraits

Colonial Williamsburg did not set out to create a notable collection of early paintings. Instead, we sought good portraits of prominent eighteenth-century Virginians and other canvases appropriate to Williamsburg.

As an important by-product of this effort, we have acquired half a dozen masterpieces with significant historical associations, portraits of Washington, Jefferson, and James Madison by Gilbert Stuart; Patrick Henry, by Thomas Sully; Speaker John Robinson, by John Wollaston; Edmund Pendleton, attributed to Charles Willson Peale. Rather than use these portraits in our period rooms we have grouped them in the Conference Room of the Capitol, where they make a most effective contribution to the interpretation of Virginia's revolutionary history. Artists and subjects have combined to make a visit to this single room in the Capitol one of the most memorable in the Williamsburg experience.

Numerous important artists passed through Williamsburg in the eighteenth century, and some of their work is now displayed here. In addition to Charles Willson Peale and John Wollaston, these included Charles Bridges, John Hesselius, Matthew Pratt, and William Dering, whose works in our collection range from the Princeton portrait of Washington to the appealing likeness of Anne Byrd, daughter of the celebrated Colonel William Byrd II.

Lord Botetourt's inventory included portraits of the king and queen in the Palace ballroom, and so George III and his consort Queen Charlotte, painted by Allen Ramsey, now hang there. Lord Dunmore listed among his Williamsburg furnishings "a number of valuable pictures by Sir Peter Lely," as well as some "costly prints." We have no way of knowing precisely what these were, but examples of Lely's work are now in the Palace.

Prints of the twelve Caesars—a popular tavern subject—have been returned to the Raleigh Tavern, just as they were specified in the inventory of innkeeper Anthony Hay, and the well-known Fry and Jefferson map of Virginia is now seen in the parlor of the Palace. Our collection of some three thousand English and American eighteenth-century prints and maps is an invaluable reference for scholars.

In addition to numerous items found in traditional collections, Colonial Williamsburg has acquired a diversity of other antiques. Firearms range from fine sporting guns such as Lord Dunmore once owned to military-issue Brown Bess muskets. There are scientific instruments such as were used by Professor George Wythe. The collections of books are based on inventories of personal libraries, such as those of Lord Botetourt and Peyton Randolph, which we painstakingly reassembled, largely through searches in London's rare-book shops.

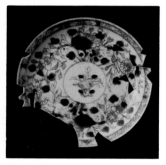

This saucer of Chinese porcelain was excavated during archaeological work at Henry Wetherburn's Tavern in 1965. It could have been one of the "6 Enameled cups and Saucers..." listed among his goods in 1760.

There is an impressive collection of musical instruments, including organs and harpsichords and virtually all forms of stringed, percussion, and wind instruments known to eighteenth-century Williamsburg. The Palace concerts provide a dramatic example of the interpretation and use of these instruments. The musicians regularly use such instruments as a Kirckman harpsichord, made in London about 1765; a viola by Gasparo de Salo, Brescia, 1560-70; Italian violins by Carlo Testore, Milan, 1698, and Tomasso Balestrieri, Mantua, 1757; and a violoncello by Peter Wormsley, London, about 1740.

Other specialized groups include artisans' tools, over 2,500 alone from the collection formed by Stephen C. Wolcott and given to Colonial Williamsburg.

Among miscellaneous items are game counters and leather jugs, wigs and horn cups. The list is virtually endless.

Though our collections have grown rapidly over the years as our knowledge has expanded, we realize that our work is far from complete.

Unfinished Business

A major undertaking now in progress is the development of Carter's Grove as a working plantation of the eighteenth century. This majestic original country house, six miles from Williamsburg on the banks of the James River, has been praised by the architectural critic Samuel Chamberlain as "the most beautiful house in America." It was acquired through the leadership of Winthrop Rockefeller and the generosity of his brothers. The current development of Carter's Grove in the pattern of a working plantation of the eighteenth century will enrich our interpretation of life in Williamsburg—which was from its beginning the political and social center of a developing agricultural empire of vast dimensions. Soon, for the first time, visitors will be able to sense the intimate relationships between productive plantations and the small capital. This, we believe, will fill one of the most important gaps in our interpretation of life in colonial Virginia.

The extensive program of research into the daily life of early plantations already launched is so ambitious that it has taken our research staff into different fields—of horticulture, animal husbandry, agriculture, and transatlantic trade.

The sixteen handsome rooms of Carter's Grove will provide striking settings for the appropriate furnishings to be displayed here. The architectural historian Hugh Morrison, in his book, *Early American Architecture*, said of the pine-paneled entrance hall: "This room is a masterpiece—early Georgian brought to its finest maturity." The furnishings program here will place new demands on our curatorial staff. For this purpose we will seek appropriate antique furnishings from generous friends of Williamsburg.

Also among our future plans is the creation of a separate museum of fine antique furnishings and archaeology, spanning two centuries. The concept of this museum, which could be located on the perimeter of the Historic Area, has been approved by Colonial Williamsburg's trustees. It would provide for the exhibition of superlative examples of English and American decorative arts under one roof and cast further light on the furnishings program of Colonial Williamsburg. Here, for instance, will be seen the Tompion clock and the William III silver chandelier, both inspiring objects, but not such as would have been seen, we now believe, in the Williamsburg of the eighteenth century. The museum will also house archaeological displays and will periodically offer special exhibitions—of eighteenth-century Virginia furnishings, for example. In these ways the museum will supplement the present program and broaden its educational effort.

The Abby Aldrich Rockefeller Folk Art Collection

Colonial Williamsburg has a related museum not solely concerned with eighteenth-century Virginia life, the Abby Aldrich Rockefeller Folk Art Collection. In the late 1920s and early 1930s Mrs. Rockefeller, a pioneer collector of American folk art,

Attributed to Wilhelm Schimmel, this wooden eagle from the Abby Aldrich Rockefeller Folk Art Collection was carved during the last quarter of the nineteenth century.

acquired more than four hundred important objects which she loaned to Colonial Williamsburg in 1935 and later donated.

Her collection included outstanding examples of sculpture—weather vanes, shop signs, ships' carvings, and garden figures; portraits, landscapes, and genre scenes depicting aspects of everyday American life—in oil, watercolor, and pastel—on canvas, cloth, and paper; "school girl" art, particularly theorem or stencil paintings and mourning pictures. This important and unique assemblage of folk art formed the nucleus for the present collection; it now numbers more than 2,000 principal objects, including calligraphic drawings and fracturs, wood and metal sculpture, toys, painted furniture and decorative household items, quilts and coverlets. The collection continues to grow through gifts and purchases.

Housed next to the Historic Area, this museum provides a year-round program of changing exhibitions, gallery tours, publications, and films, and exhibits its paintings, sculpture, and decorated useful wares so that visitors may gain fresh insight into the lives of Americans of the eighteenth and nineteenth centuries.

Nineteenth-Century Antiques

As the two hundredth anniversary of the removal of Virginia's capital from Williamsburg to Richmond nears, we realize more clearly that the lessons Colonial Williamsburg has to offer did not end with the eighteenth century. Therefore, we are moving forward in certain aspects of our program into the nineteenth century. We have begun by restoring and furnishing the Coke-Garrett House (an important original building) as the official residence of the president of the Foundation. Since the various parts of this house were built from 1755 to 1837, this new approach enabled the curatorial staff to furnish the house with a small but representative group of nineteenth-century objects too late for use in our eighteenth-century buildings. We hope to expand our collections in this period, so that the curators can study the whole range of decorative arts, without being restricted to the seventeenth and eighteenth centuries.

Donors to the Collection

Colonial Williamsburg continues to accept with gratitude donations of period antiques to enrich this unusual collection, which has been built by the cooperative efforts of so many people. These donors, far too numerous to mention here by name, have entrusted Colonial Williamsburg with many precious collections, most of them acquired during lifetimes of concentrated effort. They have played a major role in our progress, and I believe that these friends have joined us because they see clearly the underlying purpose of our existence. Without their aid the Foundation could hardly have assembled, as a contribution to the national heritage, this city-wide re-creation of a formative era from our past. The generous people who have joined in this effort share with us the conviction that the restoration of this setting does much to inspire modern Americans with the stirring accomplishments of the remarkable Virginians who helped to found our nation.

Looking back over almost fifty years of the assembly of these fine antique furnishings, I am deeply impressed by the wisdom and foresight of Mr. Rockefeller, Jr. From the very beginning he sensed the importance of the collection of period furnishings in telling the story of Colonial Williamsburg and bringing to life its eventful past. His insistence upon the building of a collection of the highest quality has created a major cultural asset for the American people.

—CARLISLE H. HUMELSINE
President, The Colonial Williamsburg Foundation

In the following pages Curator Graham Hood and a staff
of trained and experienced specialists present a series of
interiors and objects from the Colonial Williamsburg collection.
The objects pictured, some two thousand in number, were
selected by Mr. Hood as representative of the more than one
hundred thousand under his care. For a closer acquaintance with
this superb collection, readers are invited to
view it firsthand in Williamsburg.

The Governor's Palace

The Governor's Palace served as the official residence of seven royal governors and the first two elected governors of the commonwealth of Virginia—Patrick Henry and Thomas Jefferson. A spacious complex, consisting of a large central building and numerous outbuildings, it was completed about 1720 and extended in 1750-51. Its style and form influenced much of Virginia's later architecture, and the Palace became a symbol of the prosperity of the flourishing agricultural economy. It was destroyed by fire in 1781 and rose again above its old foundations in 1932 after extensive and productive archaeological, architectural, and historical research.

The colony provided "standing furniture" for the Palace, but most of its furnishings were the personal property of the governor, either imported from England or bought from his predecessor. Documentation for the contents of this handsome building includes an appraisal of the late Governor Fauquier's effects in 1768; and, most important, the detailed inventory of the possessions of Lord Botetourt, the penultimate royal governor, taken in 1770 after his sudden death. This highly significant cultural document about the life of the ruling class in the colonies has been used as a guide in determining the functions of various rooms and in furnishing them. There is also an inventory left by Botetourt's successor, Lord Dunmore, based on his claim to the British government for household goods appropriated by the colonists during the Revolution. Two floors and basement of the main building and the ground floors of the flanking buildings are now exhibited, as well as the kitchen, smokehouse, laundry, and stables.

Specified as the "front parlour" in the Botetourt inventory, this room then contained eleven Chelsea china figures and two brass "branches" (sconces), seen here reflected in the looking glass at the left. "Thirty-four Scripture prints," two looking glasses, and three large maps were also listed—one map is visible, rolled up in the corner. Two mahogany card tables, a walnut writing table, nine chairs, and a couch were included in this room. The English chandelier is a fine example dating from the 1760s.

Chinoiserie-style settee made in England entirely of mahogany, about 1760–70. Before the Revolution, it came into the possession of the Wentworth family of Portsmouth, New Hampshire—a family that provided the two royal governors for that colony in the eighteenth century, Benning and his nephew John.

Standing across the hall from the parlor is a room of equal size shown with a Christmas setting of candied and fresh fruits in English delft containers. The magnificent English silver chandelier (p. 114) complements the commanding Philadelphia tall-case clock in the Chippendale style, with works made by Edward Duffield about 1760-75.

By tradition, part of the furnishings of Ham House in London, this one of a pair of *torchères* was made there in the last quarter of the seventeenth century. Almost four feet high, it is decorated with silver gesso on deal, oak, and walnut.

[21]

The focal point of the dining room table is an English silver epergne, made by Thomas Pitts in 1762 in fanciful Chinese pagoda shape. While no such form is specified in the Botetourt inventory, several are recorded in Virginia, including one owned by Thomas Nelson of Yorktown. Lord Botetourt used great quantities of silver and glass at the Palace. An excellent English looking glass in the rococo taste hangs between Genoese cut-velvet curtains of about 1700—the winter set for this room.

Exquisite silver-gilt salver made by Thomas Farren in London about 1730 for the royal collection; 13⅜ inches long. Four salvers and a large tea board are included in the list of plate in the Botetourt inventory.

A second glimpse of this splendid room—a view not normally seen by the visitor. Eleven more Chelsea china figures, like those listed here in 1770, line the mantelpiece above a summer arrangement for the fireplace. Dumbwaiters bearing cruets, sauce boats, tureens, extra plates, and utensils for serving wine and beer are shown pulled up to the table. Although the inventory mentions a "large oil cloth," the eighteenth-century Turkish carpet here is similar to the one shown in the mid-century English "conversation piece" above the serving table. Botetourt owned several knife-and-fork boxes and also a silver bread basket—examples of these are shown on the serving table.

One of a pair of standing knife boxes made of sheet iron, painted and gilded, of the type normally called Pontypool. Made about 1760, they are 16½ inches high.

An exceptional silver-gilt bread basket in the rococo taste, one of a pair, made in London in 1747-48 by Paul de Lamerie and engraved with the Sneyd arms.

[23]

The Botetourt inventory itemized "56 pieces ornamental China" and "2 pr English China candlesticks" in the "bowfat" in the dining room. The English Chippendale-style bookcase desk here serves to display "ornamental" Chelsea porcelain of the early periods and of the finest quality—an allusion to the "English China" mentioned above and the Chelsea figures already seen in this room. The bust, also Chelsea, probably represents George III.

Silver-gilt wine fountain, 24⅝ inches high, made by Joseph Ward in London, 1702–3. Among many other things, the Council, in 1710, proposed to furnish the Governor's Palace with "one Marble Buffette or sideboard with a Cistern & fountain."

Five glass chandeliers were described in the Botetourt inventory as hanging (some with gauze covers) in the ballroom and supper room; they are also documented as having been moved to Richmond by Jefferson in 1780. The portraits of the king and queen in the ballroom in Botetourt's time were also equipped with gauze covers, presumably to guard against the swarms of flies coming in through the unscreened windows. Lord Dunmore listed several fine paintings by Lely, possibly such portraits of Charles II and his queen as are shown here. He also had three organs, a harpsichord, and a pianoforte—contemporary examples of these are normally exhibited. Botetourt kept forty-seven chairs in these two rooms alone! This view shows the summer hangings and check covers for chair seats so popular at the time.

Made about 1665 in England, this so-called "stumpwork" embroidered casket appears to have been given by Charles II to James Whitton, ranger of Woodstock, Oxford. Its wooden frame is decorated with tortoise shell, parchment, linen, silk, brass, and pearls, among other things. It is 9¼ inches high.

Behind the wire-grill doors of this magisterial bookcase in the "Passage up Stairs" are most of the 311 titles that constituted Lord Botetourt's library. The breakfront bookcase was made, possibly by Thomas Chippendale, in the late 1760s and came from Nostell Priory, Yorkshire, England. It is documented that Botetourt kept at least some of his books behind curtains. The closet off this passage contained, among other things "24 pounds of chocolate... and five toothbrushes."

An excellent Philadelphia Chippendale upholstered armchair, possibly made by Thomas Affleck, stands before a superb Massachusetts Chippendale *bombé* chest-on-chest in the "Chamber over the Dining Room." A "Sheffield-ware tea kitchen," such as the Botetourt inventory itemized, occupies the tea table in the center of the room. Also mentioned in the inventory are the oak bedstead, the looking glass with two sconces, and "one mahogany desk empty," visible here on the left. What we have not yet found are the "eight green bamboo chairs with check'd cushions" that were here in 1770 (four more were in the governor's bedchamber). In the summer, the bed is hung with "muscato curtains," as used by the governor.

Bombé chest-on-chest made in Massachusetts in the Chippendale style.
Mahogany with white pine. Height: 91¾ inches.

Rich, elaborate, and beautiful, this bookcase was made of rosewood
and mahogany in London about 1760; 106 inches in height.

Exuberant in design and of exquisite quality, one of a pair of silver sconces made in London in 1700-1701 by Philip Rollos, and engraved with the cypher of William III; 15¾ inches high.

Fine, white Chelsea porcelain, including a bust of the duke of Cumberland—a friend of Lord Botetourt's—and English silver sconces adorn the fireplace wall of the "Chamber over the Front Parlour." Botetourt owned six silver sconces, two even with "four nozzles each"—extremely rare. The bed is furnished with an early eighteenth-century adjustable back rest and a tray carrying medical paraphernalia of glass, silver, and pottery. The late seventeenth-century English invalid's chair, on which the back and foot adjust together by means of leather straps, is a most unusual item.

"Two long looking glasses with red gilded frames" and a "glass lustre with six branches" adorned the "Middle Room" in 1770. "Four gilded brackets" and "eight crimson damask chairs with red check covers" added further elegance. Shown here in the center of the room is an imposing jewel casket of tortoise shell, mother-of-pearl, and silver probably made in Jamaica about 1700. It was presented to Colonial Williamsburg by Queen Elizabeth II.

Pillow cover of linen, patterned with silk embroidery and cord quilting, English, early eighteenth century.

The manservant has laid out the morning's clothes (including a gentleman's fan) and waits in "His Lordship's Bed Chamber" for the governor to finish his toilet in the adjoining closet. Specified in the 1770 inventory are the mahogany bedstead with green hangings and "one small chest of draws, some stockings and caps." The shoe buckles, "one wash bason and mahogany stand compleat with a dressing glass," and the silver chamber pot seen beneath the window in the closet are also listed. The eighteenth-century carpet is Caucasian.

The governor reads to his lady in the quiet of this informal interior, possibly the "Library" listed in the 1770 inventory. Decorated with eighteenth-century Chinese wallpaper, it contains an outstanding early eighteenth-century English wing chair covered in original tent-stitch embroidery and an equally fine Philadelphia Chippendale commode chair. On the desk in the foreground is shown a lovely all-white figure of the goddess "Cybele," made in England of Derby porcelain in the 1750s. The tall-case clock and the fowling piece in the closet have a tradition of ownership by Lord Dunmore.

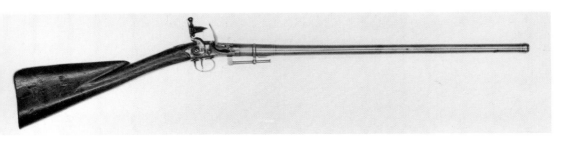

Engraved with the Dunmore arms, this breech-loading rifle was made by W. Hutchinson in England about 1740.

[33]

Unknown lady seated at a table on which lie watercolors, a "drawing box," and her artistic efforts, painted about 1750 by Arthur Devis (1711–87). English, oil on canvas, 22⅝ x 16¾ inches.

This pair of Chelsea porcelain baskets is marked with a raised anchor and was made about 1750-53. They are 8⅝ inches long.

Of especial note in the governor's office, located in the East Advance Building, is the wing chair with a reclining back, its original leather upholstery cut at the borders to simulate lace. The marquetry desk is English of the late seventeenth century and the Staffordshire pottery busts are of King George III and Queen Charlotte. It seems to have been a common eighteenth-century practice for chair covers to fit as loosely as the red-check example here.

Peyton Randolph House

The home of an accomplished member of
one of Virginia's most powerful
families and president of the First
Continental Congress, the Peyton Randolph House was built about 1715 and extended
later. An imposing original building, it contains one of the best series of paneled rooms in
Williamsburg. On Peyton Randolph's death in 1775 an inventory was taken of his
possessions. Mrs. Randolph's will, written shortly afterwards, gives details of sophisticated
items, such as silver and Chelsea porcelain, that did not appear in the inventory. The
furnishings are based on these documents, and reflect the high position in society that the
Randolphs occupied, as well as Mr. Randolph's travels in this country and in England.

William Byrd II recorded that Charles Bridges painted his daughter Anne as a young girl at Westover in 1735. This portrait (57 x 47 inches) thus has the most convincing attribution to Bridges of any picture. It remained in the possession of the Byrd and Carter families until acquired by Colonial Williamsburg.

Prints frequently appear in contemporary illustrations to be hung ascending the hall staircase—as is this mezzotint set of *The Months*. Below the first landing is a colored set of *The Seasons*, eighteenth-century English copies of seventeenth-century Dutch paintings, enclosed in one antique frame. Using a scallop shell and a straw to blow bubbles, as the little girl is doing inside on a rainy day, is documented in other paintings of the period.

Tea in the parlor, using the "Chelsea china tea set" that Mrs. Randolph mentioned in her will, served from a fine Massachusetts Queen Anne tea table. Two tea tables were specified in the 1776 inventory of Peyton Randolph's estate and two tea sets in his wife's will, the other being of "India China." On either side of mantel, on ornate gilt shelves, are precious small-scale pieces comparable to the "sett of ornamental china" highly valued in the inventory. To the right of the fireplace is the rare, original leather box for the mid-eighteenth century English silver tea kettle on stand. And if such were ever needed, there is direct pictorial evidence that cookies were as appealing to little boys in the eighteenth century as they are now.

Arranged for the midday dinner that was customary in the colonial period, the table is dominated by a rare Bow porcelain tureen of about 1750–60. Silver candlesticks in both the old and the new styles are specified in Mrs. Randolph's will of 1780. Two silver salvers on the marble-topped serving table and the beaker on the mantelpiece bear the Randolph arms. In the fireplace stands an unusual English Chippendale-style portable grate of brass. New England Queen Anne chairs and Chelsea porcelain painted with botanical themes complete the ensemble. Forty-eight tablecloths, but only nine napkins, appear in the inventory—and no paintings. We know from other sources that the Randolphs owned portraits.

Red stoneware coffeepot bearing a factory mark in the Chinese manner. Probably Staffordshire, mid-eighteenth century.

One of two small silver salvers made by William Peaston in London, 1753-55. Engraved with the Randolph family crest, they were originally owned by Peyton Randolph and are listed as "2 Silver Waiters" in Mrs. Randolph's will.

Antique furnishings in the study of the busy lawyer and politician include the late seventeenth-century English needlework upholstery and the early eighteenth-century English desk, both of bold form and detail; the brass and silver accoutrements on the desk, especially the huge silver-rimmed magnifying glass held here; and the cards the little girl is absorbed in. Two painted canvas floorcloths are listed in the inventory.

A finely engraved brass box for writing implements, made in Sheffield and dated 1655. It is 5⅛ inches long.

A game or puzzle published by John Wallis in 1788; in a mahogany box 3¼ inches long.

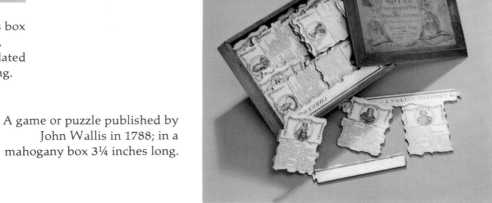

This plain but pleasing mahogany clothespress was made in Williamsburg. It is closely related in style to other examples owned locally. Stored above are a tricorn hat box and a traveling trunk. All date from the eighteenth-century.

English needlework carpet of about 1740; 122 inches long.

Tea tray or "tea board," beautifully made of mahogany in England about 1760; 22½ inches long.

Enhancing the fine Newport Chippendale bed in the west bedroom are English, eighteenth-century printed cotton hangings with scenes from Bickerstaff's *The Padlock,* an opera performed in Williamsburg in 1771. Cotton and light-weight linen were most suitable for the predominantly warm Virginia climate. So great was the need for such materials that domestically-made types appeared—this inventory lists several beds with suits of "Virginia cloth," one with matching window curtains. An important Massachusetts Chippendale bureau and an outstanding Philadelphia Queen Anne chair here reflect the quality of the Randolphs' station in life.

Superb walnut Philadelphia Queen Anne side chair. Owned by the Coates and Reynell families until acquired by Colonial Williamsburg recently.

Finely detailed Massachusetts tea table made in the Queen Anne style of mahogany and white pine. Said to have been owned in South Hingham, Massachusetts, in the late eighteenth-century.

Dominating the oak-paneled bedroom is the veneered, New England Queen Anne dressing table of outstanding quality. One of the few known Philadelphia low-post, ball-and-claw-foot beds is also here. The Dutch brass footwarmer would have been a common sight in Williamsburg, as would the medical equipment on the dressing table. Light-weight wools that the English made in prodigious quantities were widely appreciated in Virginia for such items as coats, curtains, or cushions. Clothes consumed much of the quantity; they wore out more frequently and fashions for them changed much more often than for furnishings.

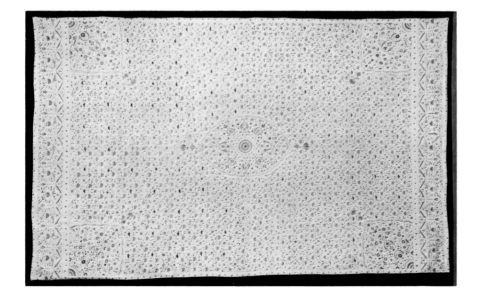

Silk coverlet patterned with polychrome silk embroidery, made in England in the first quarter of the eighteenth century; 114 inches long. It was to such people as the Randolphs that the great quantities of variegated silks were dispatched from Europe. Their value was frequently calculated in so many pounds of tobacco, and so purchased. Again, they could be used for upholstery or dress purposes.

This interior, like many others shown here, is based on an English eighteenth-century painting (see p. 34). A number of objects of English origin and from the second half of the eighteenth century are to be found in the east bedroom: the needlework carpet, the wing chair with its original brocaded Norwich wool, the copper coal scuttle, the steel and brass matching fender and grate, and the portrait by Francis Cotes. Of American origin and from the same period are the Pennsylvania high chest and the Virginia side chair next to it. An English print of the 1760s provided the precedent for the curtain arrangement.

Watercolor paint or "drawing" box sold in London in the 1780s by Thomas Reeves & Son. The box is walnut and some of the paints are of the period; 8½ inches long.

Summer in the same room calls for the grass mat that was common in the eighteenth century and recommended for coolness and light-colored seersucker curtains instead of the dark blue silk damask. The crewel bed hangings are of American origin, as is the bed itself (Massachusetts) and the chest of drawers (Philadelphia), all made in the second half of the eighteenth century. The dressing table arrangement also derives from pictorial sources of the period.

Back panel of crewel-embroidered bedhangings, made in New England in the mid-eighteenth century; 70¾ inches.

George Wythe House

Built about mid-century by his father-in-law and inhabited by George Wythe until 1790, this brick mansion represents an engaging local version of the English Georgian style. Wythe's intellectual pursuits typify those of the colonial Virginia gentry—science, philosophy, law, and husbandry, although his position as the first professor of law at the College of William and Mary and his interest in teaching mark him as exceptional. His house and its dependencies followed the typical plantation scheme (without, of course the vast land holdings characteristic of the colonial plantation) and are furnished to illustrate his particular interests as well as the mode of life of a representative Virginia gentleman. The building is original.

Eighteenth-century inventories frequently listed large sets of chairs in "the passage"; the straight-forward, sturdy, and rather appealing "leather-bottomed" walnut chairs seen in this handsome stair hall are of Virginia origin. Above the excellent New York Chippendale gate-leg table is the Charles Willson Peale portrait of Nancy Hallam playing the role of Imogen in Shakespeare's *Cymbeline.* Both artist and subject were in Williamsburg just before the Revolution, Peale in 1774. Shortly afterwards he painted a battle flag for the Independent Company of Williamsburg.

One of the earliest paintings connected with the American theatre, this portrait of Nancy Hallam was painted by Charles Willson Peale in 1771, apparently for his own collection. He exhibited it at the Annapolis Theatre during a performance of *Cymbeline* in that year. Oil on canvas, 50 x 40 inches. A fellow student of Benjamin West's, Matthew Pratt, held an exhibition of his paintings in Williamsburg in 1773 at Mrs. Vobe's, later the King's Arms Tavern. One of the paintings shown there, a rare American allegory of "Europa and the Bull," has recently been placed on long-term loan at Colonial Williamsburg.

To paraphrase *The Beggars' Opera*, "a pretty girl is ever worth regarding. . . ." Flanking the window of the parlor is a pair of English, early eighteenth-century, japanned looking glasses, of fine quality. The carpet is Caucasian ("dragon" Kuba), while the chair to the left represents the Philadelphia Chippendale style at its pinnacle.

Outstanding mahogany side chair (tulip poplar secondary wood) made probably by Benjamin Randolph of Philadelphia in the third quarter of the eighteenth century.

The rare and exceptionally fine Leeds creamware centerpiece in the dining room dates from the 1770s. George Wythe almost certainly used creamware here, as he lived in the house until 1790. The plates and bonbon dishes match the *platte de menage.*

The built-in buffet in the dining room contains English porcelain and polychrome saltglazed stoneware. On the bottom shelf stand a Chinese blue-and-white tea set and eighteenth-century English glass and silver. Many fragments of engraved eighteenth-century English decanters and wine glasses have been brought to light by Colonial Williamsburg's archaeologists.

[49]

Surviving correspondence has revealed that Wythe ordered a brass telescope from London; fragments of such an instrument as seen here have been found in local archaeological excavations. The scientific instruments, the important sea chart above the fireplace (done on vellum in the eighteenth century from a seventeenth-century map and hung on rollers in characteristic fashion), and the print of *The Alchemist* from the Wright of Derby painting, all attest to the nature of Wythe's intellect. To the left of the window of the students' room is a print of *The Observer* by Thomas Frye, exactly the kind documented as being in colonial Williamsburg. The English early eighteenth-century gate-leg table with Spanish feet is one of extremely fine quality.

A rare air pump probably by William Cary. The wooden frame is mahogany; the other fittings are of brass and glass. Made in England, 1785–1800. Height: 15¼ inches.

The wife of a Virginia merchant, Mrs. Gavin Lawson was painted by John Hesselius in 1770. The painting is signed. Oil on canvas, 49¾ x 39 inches. John Wollaston had been painting portraits in the Williamsburg area in the 1750s and a number of examples of his work are shown in the Wythe House.

The Observer, drawn and engraved by Thomas Frye in 1760; 20 x 14¼ inches.

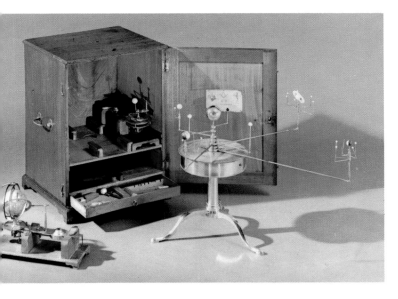

Brass orrery in a walnut case, signed by W. & S. Jones of Holborn, London, about 1770. Height: 22 inches.

A standing barometer signed by Daniel Quare, made in London about 1700. The only known example of a barometer with the shaft covered in sharkskin. Height: 40 inches.

A huge southern clothespress dominates the northwest bedroom. Also seen here is a "list," or rag-woven carpet, of the kind recorded in Virginia from the 1760s onward.

Similar to fragments excavated locally, this transfer-printed creamware basket and stand were made in the Staffordshire area of England about 1780.

The German bleats & bares ye Furs | Th Hibernian frets with new Disaster | But help at hand Resolves to hold down
Of Quaker Lords & Savage Curs | And kicks to flinghis broad brim'd Master | Th Hibernian's Head or tumble all down

Benjamin Franklin visited Williamsburg and received an honorary degree at the College of William and Mary shortly before this political satiric print of him was made. A rare American example of this type of engraving, it was probably executed by James Claypoole, Jr., in Philadelphia about 1764. It measures 7⅛ x 9⅞ inches.

Silk damask made in France or Italy, mid-eighteenth century; 20¾ inches wide.

December from Burford's glass transfer prints of the months, made in London 1745–47; 14 x 9⅛ inches.

Revealing the Wythe House and its outbuildings as an urban plantation-type complex, this view further shows some early gardening implements. The roller, rake, fork, trug basket, watering can, and wheelbarrow are eighteenth century in form or origin; the bell jar is later. Colonial examples, well documented in Williamsburg, were of dark green bottle glass and more flared. We are still searching for such an item.

Brocaded wool damask made in Norwich, England, 1760–75; 28½ inches wide.

The list of subscribers who supported the making and publication of Robert Furber's *Twelve Months of Flowers* in London in 1730. Drawn by Ptr. Casteels and engraved by H. Fletcher.

Brush-Everard House

Smaller and considerably less formal than the preceding houses, the Brush-Everard House was built in 1717 by John Brush, a gunsmith, and extended after 1750. Pleasing architectural details, such as the staircase, with its carved brackets, add distinction to this modestly-sized, original house. Two schedules for a deed of mortgage in 1744–45 indicate how the house was furnished before Thomas Everard acquired it. The present furnishings attempt to reflect Everard's position as clerk of the York County Court and mayor of Williamsburg in 1766 and 1771.

A fine southern buffet of the second half of the eighteenth century exhibits part of a remarkable collection of polychrome, salt-glazed stoneware from Staffordshire. The covered tankard at the lower right commemorates the capture of Porto Bello in 1739, and is uncommon. From archaeological evidence it is apparent that the common undecorated wares abounded in colonial Williamsburg. Since they were never so highly valued and were more often discarded, they are among the most difficult-to-find antiques today.

Tall-case clock of walnut, with chestnut and yellow pine secondary woods, made 1770-85. The works are signed by Thomas Walker of Fredericksburg, Virginia.

An extremely rare view of Charleston, South Carolina, painted in watercolor on paper by Bishop Roberts about 1739; 15 x 43⅜ inches.

Above the strikingly modeled block-front, walnut desk from Delaware, made about 1750-75, hangs the signed and dated portrait of Mrs. Elizabeth Stith, painted by William Dering who lived here in the 1740s.

The mahogany low-post bed with maple rails was probably made in Massachusetts or Rhode Island, 1760-90. It is the only known American bed incorporating carved busts on the posts. The spread is resist-dyed linen and cotton, made in France in the mid-eighteenth century.

Cotton, resist-dyed in indigo either in America or in England, at the end of the eighteenth century; 35¼ inches wide.

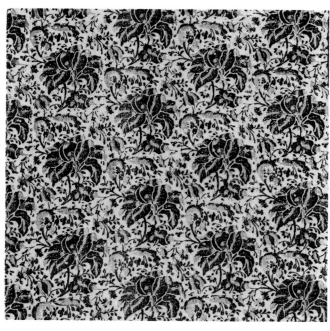

Cotton, copperplate-printed in blue at Bromley Hall, England, about 1775; 28½ inches wide.

Fine pistol by R. Silke, made about 1670 in London; 20 inches long.

A rare tortoise-shell-colored cruet stand of earthenware. Probably made at Leeds, England, about 1765. Height: 10 inches.

This charming original kitchen has dirt floors. It is shown here equipped with the necessarily wide range of cooking utensils of pewter, brass, copper, iron, and pottery; all are of the colonial period.

The stables of the Ludwell-Paradise house are here replete with leather equipment for horses and such mechanical implements as a coach jack. The vehicle outside is comparable to the "well-built handsome post-charriott" that George Wythe ordered from London in 1768.

The Capitol

For most of the eighteenth century—from 1704 until 1780—the largest colony in British America was governed from two successive capitol buildings at the eastern end of the Duke of Gloucester Street. Executive, judicial, and legislative power was concentrated here. On this site in 1765 Patrick Henry stirred the colonies with his denunciation of the Stamp Act, and a little more than ten years later rebellious leaders passed the Virginia Resolves, calling for American independence, then adopted a new state constitution and elected Henry governor. Today's building, furnished in keeping with its formal, official functions, adds much to the interpretation of this important place in American history. In the House of Burgesses, where America's oldest representative assembly met, stands the eighteenth-century Speaker's chair. An excellent collection of portraits of leaders of Virginia's revolutionary movement hangs in the Conference Room on the second floor.

George Washington would have been familiar with the General Court Room, seen through the door. The monumental portrait of him as a military hero, with Princeton in the background, was painted by Charles Willson Peale in Philadelphia in 1780 on bedticking. Tradition has it that Washington presented the portrait to his friend and ally, Governor Thomas Nelson of Yorktown, whose daughter married Robert Carter of Shirley plantation, where it remained until this century. A later period of Peale's art is superbly represented in our collections by the portraits of Mr. Robert Gilmor, Baltimore merchant, and his wife, dated 1785.

Evoking the constitutional conflicts between royal government and local representation, the House of Burgesses is dominated by the Speaker's chair. Although "a large armed chair" had been ordered for the Speaker in 1703, it probably did not survive the fire of 1747. Almost certainly this chair was built for the second Capitol, completed in 1753. A visitor to Williamsburg described it and made a sketch of it in 1777. Three years later it was moved to Richmond with the rest of the state possessions and remained there until recent years. Through the courtesy of the General Assembly of Virginia it was returned to the Capitol in Williamsburg.

A rare engraving of *The Three Cherokees, came over from the head of the River Savanna to London 1762.* The three Indians had expressed a wish to "see the king my father," and the print (9⅜ x 11¾ inches) was made shortly after their visit to London. The Indian was a particular and continuing concern to colonial authorities, often requiring special legislation.

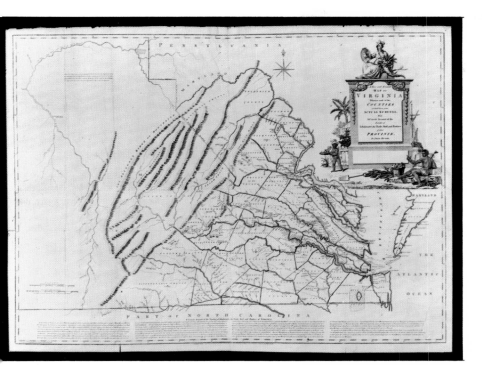

A New and Accurate Map of Virginia . . . made by John Henry and engraved by Thomas Jefferys in London, dated February, 1770, 38¼ x 51½ inches. The boundaries are hand-colored. Such maps were among the requisites of colonial governments in determining boundaries of colonies and counties.

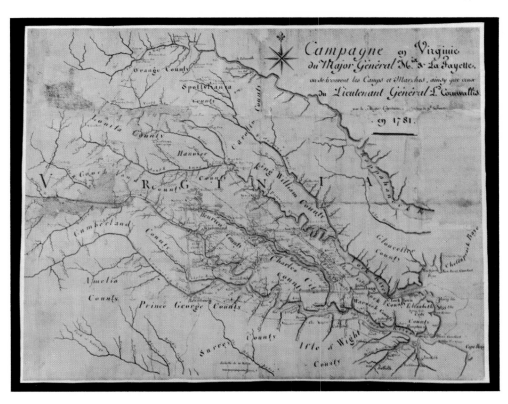

Manuscript map of the marquis de Lafayette's campaign in Virginia, dated 1781—a unique and important document; 35 x 44 inches.

"Vaughan-type" portrait of President Washington by Gilbert Stuart, 1795, of exceptional quality. Oil on canvas, 29 x 24¼ inches.

Portrait of Patrick Henry painted by Thomas Sully from a miniature in 1815. It descended in the Henry family until this century. Oil on canvas, 30 x 25 inches.

Thomas Jefferson, brilliantly painted by Gilbert Stuart about 1805. Oil on canvas, 30 x 25 inches.

The many Williamsburg interiors are used for a variety of educational purposes. In this scene from the well-known orientation film *Williamsburg—The Story of a Patriot,* Governor Dunmore has summoned the burgesses to the Council Chamber and dissolved the House.

From the journal of the House of Burgesses, 1703, it is known "that there be provided to be set in the Council Chamber one oval table 14 foot long and six foot broad with two doz: arm'd Cain Chairs, 1 larger ditto, twenty-five green Cushions for the said Chairs stuft with hair, and a large Turkey-work Carpet for the table." In the following year were ordered "six brass Candlesticks & two pair of Snuffers and Snuff dishes, two Chamber Potts, 4 Standishes, 6 brass Sconces each to hold two Candles, 6 large Penknives, some Recording Ink, 6 Pieces of red tape, 6 Pieces of broad tape, some blue, red & green ribbon for stitching the Council Journals." The same order included "a Callico Curtaine to hang before the Queen's Picture." The Council ordered payment to Sir Godfrey Kneller for the queen's portrait in this year.

James Geddy House

Built about mid-century, this original house and its attendant shops reflect many of the occupations practiced there in the third quarter of the eighteenth century—gunsmith, founder, cutler, blacksmith, silversmith, jeweler, engraver, watch finisher, and import merchant. Although an inventory exists for James Geddy, the gunsmith, dated 1744, no similar document has been found for his son, also James Geddy, the best-known silversmith in town until he moved away in 1777.

Eighteenth-century English silversmiths' tools on the walls and shelves and the Paul Revere anvil near the craftsman play important parts in our interpretation of a colonial craft. The children's toys are of the period, also.

Lancaster County, Pennsylvania, long rifle signed J. S[t]ock, and dated 1774. Length: 61 inches.

The large southern buffet in the parlor contains delftware, glass, salt-glazed stoneware, and Wedgwood-Whieldon ware, all exactly paralleling items that were used here.

Parts of a tea service, each piece in the form of a cauliflower, made in Staffordshire of lead-glazed earthenware about 1765.

A built-in cupboard in the Geddy parlor displays the types of wares and forms of which fragments were found in the course of archaeological excavation around the house. Wedgwood-Whieldon, Jackfield, dry-bodied redwares, and the printed creamware plates at the top were commonly used in Williamsburg in the second half of the eighteenth century.

A lead-glazed earthenware coffeepot that may have been made by Thomas Whieldon about 1760 at Fenton Vivian, Staffordshire. Height: 6½ inches.

Brass kettle on stand, of bold form, made in England about 1725. Height: 13 inches.

Accuracy in weighing and record-keeping was essential for the eighteenth-century silversmith. On the desk in the Geddy counting room stand spoons and a brandy warmer that James Geddy made. Shoe buckles are typical of the personal adornments he sold, and the clock is of a type he could have repaired. In the cupboard are kept silver objects such as those he advertised for sale.

A Virginia bracket clock of mahogany, with works by Thomas Walker of Fredericksburg, made about 1760–75. Height: 19¾ inches.

Raleigh Tavern

This building stands on the site of the most famous of colonial taverns in Williamsburg. A center for business and pleasure, the Raleigh Tavern enjoyed extensive patronage despite the fairly frequent changes of ownership. A detailed inventory of the furnishings was taken after the death of one owner, former cabinetmaker Anthony Hay, in 1770. The present furnishings reflect that inventory closely, while their arrangement has been based largely on the plentiful prints of eighteenth-century tavern scenes.

The front passage was a bustling place of communication by letter, package, and human contact. It served for the dissemination of information, such as advertising items lost, stolen, or strayed (whether they were objects, animals, or human beings); services offered; and all manner of things for sale—including human beings. The eighteenth-century pigeon-hole cupboard is of New England origin.

One of the most popular sports (to some, a vice) in colonial Virginia was the game of billiards. A billiard table appears in the inventory of Anthony Hay. The mahogany example here is from mid-eighteenth-century England. Contemporary prints often show much diverse and stimulating visual material on the walls of such billiard rooms.

A colored stipple engraving of billiards, by Watson and Dickinson after a design by H. Bunbury. London, 1780; 11¾ x 15¼ inches.

A leather mastiff collar dated 1778, with wrought iron buckle and ring. Length: 11½ inches.

A multi-purpose room where the tavern-keeper might keep his accounts, extra supplies, odd items to be replaced or repaired, and where he could even sleep if all the other rooms were rented out. The folding bed in the left foreground shows that eighteenth-century people could be resourceful as well as elegant. The desk was probably made in Williamsburg in the colonial period, while the arm chair is a New England reeded banister-back example. A deerskin is thrown over the arm—an allusion to the mention of hides in the 1770 inventory—and the seat is patched with leather.

A signed and dated writing desk or *scrutoire* of walnut, with white cedar and white pine secondary woods, by Edward Evans of Philadelphia, 1707. Height: 66½ inches.

A room where gentlemen might retire to play cards, read the newspaper, or write letters. The important Evans desk at the left and a superb New England "mushroom arm" chair are among the notable furnishings of this room. English mid-eighteenth-century chairs complete the scene.

Ample visual evidence of how eighteenth-century tavern interiors looked and what people did in them can be found in contemporary prints. Specified in the inventory is a pine chest of drawers; the combination pine chest and desk in the taproom is a Virginia piece.

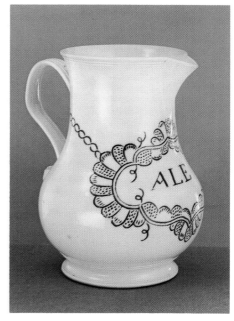

Salt-glazed stoneware jug, dated 1751, with scratch blue decoration in the form of a wine label and chain; Staffordshire. Height: 7 inches.

Tavern-keepers kept a wide range of metal, ceramic, and glass containers for serving drinks. Twenty-two china bowls were listed in 1770, and the relatively small quantity of thirty wine glasses. For the wine bottles we have countless thousands of pieces of evidence in the form of archaeological fragments.

Slip-decorated earthenware posset pot, dated 1766, from Staffordshire. Height: 9 inches.

▶

Fifty-six tables and eighty-three chairs stood in the Raleigh Tavern in 1770. The Apollo Room was a place for business—suggested by the small meeting in progress; or for pleasure—as evidenced by the game in the left foreground, the *vue d'optique* (a popular precursor of the travel film), the spinet, and the "old fiddle" in the far corner. Prints were frequently hung by different means and at different heights in eighteenth-century interiors. The great oak gate-leg table and the slender walnut chairs around it are of the finest English provincial quality and date from the first half of the eighteenth century.

The most famous of all Paul Revere's engravings, *The Bloody Massacre Perpetrated in King Street Boston on March 5th 1770, by a Party of the 29th Regt.* was engraved and hand colored in 1770 in Boston. Political prints became increasingly popular from this time onward. It is 7⅞ x 8½ inches.

Contained in the southern cupboard at the left of the Daphne Room are examples of Chinese export porcelain, Staffordshire salt-glazed stoneware, creamware, and a late Rouen faience platter—all corresponding to wares that we know were here in the eighteenth century. Thirty-seven tablecloths and sixteen napkins belonged to Anthony Hay, in addition to "10 napkins not made up." The inventory specified less than fifty lighting devices for the whole tavern.

Enameled, salt-glazed stoneware teapot from Staffordshire, about 1760. Height: 4½ inches. In Anthony Hay's inventory appear "2 large coloured stone tea potts"; these were probably single-colored rather than polychrome. Fragments of two Littler's blue teapots were excavated on the property later occupied by Anthony Hay's widow.

Solid tavern tables and Virginia chairs predominate in the public dining room. On the walls hang a set of the twelve Caesars that were popular tavern decoration in both England and the colonies and were in the tavern in 1770. The records also refer to pewter plates, leather jugs, and brass chafing dishes.

The cupboard in the public dining room provides storage for some wine glasses and part of the "412 pieces of glass for pyramids, etc." mentioned in the inventory.

White seersucker bedhangings and curtains complement the printed cotton coverlet on the right. The only window dressings mentioned in the inventory are two Venetian blinds, four pairs of window curtains, and "3 white window curtains." It is possible that the latter were of "Virginia cloth"— a "homespun" of cotton, linen, or simple combination. Travel accounts of the period relate that during busy periods strangers were obliged to share beds and as many guests were crowded into a room as possible.

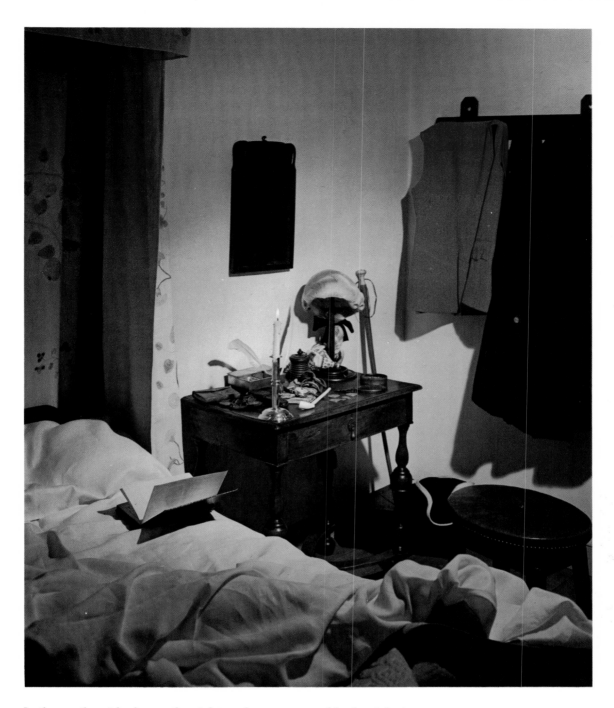

In the northeast bedroom the eighteenth-century stool in the right foreground has a tradition of being made in Virginia, and the crewelwork hangings are of American origin. On the dressing table are strewn some of the multitude of things that men might carry in their pockets.

◄

The inventory listed thirty-seven beds and twenty-three chamber pots, in addition to eighty-two blankets and eleven Dutch blankets. The quilt shown at right is an American eighteenth-century example, as is the Windsor arm chair.

Wetherburn's Tavern

An erstwhile keeper of the Raleigh, Henry Wetherburn built his own tavern and added on to it between 1740 and 1752. It has survived to this day in a remarkable state of preservation, and is furnished to accord closely with the inventory taken after Wetherburn's death in 1760. Archaeological investigations of the property have revealed extensive evidence, in addition to the inventory, of the kinds of objects used here in colonial times.

Henry Wetherburn seems to have improved himself handsomely by each of his marriages. He possessed one desk and bookcase with glass doors, eight prints, and four tables in this, the Bull's Head Room. He also owned a substantial quantity of glass and silver.

Kinds of common ware—the inventory listed them generally; the archaeologist was able to describe them precisely—exhibited in the buffet in the middle room; common then but highly collectible today.

Agate-ware milk jug of lead-glazed earthenware made in Staffordshire about 1735-50. Height: 5⁹⁄₁₆ inches.

Bristol delft mug dated 1739 and finely decorated with a painted scene of a piper and dancers in a rustic landscape. Height: 8½ inches.

Hand-colored line engraving of *Night* by J. Boydell dated 1756, London; 11⅝ x 16⅝ inches.

Cribbage board and game counter made of fruitwood, ivory, and printed paper by T. Lambe in England about 1775.

Engraving of *Subduing, Shoeing, the Cavison and Pillar*, from a series of four by W. Elliott after T. Smith, dated 1758, London; 15½ x 21⅜ inches.

Three large looking glasses and twenty-four prints and maps adorned the walls of the handsome Great Room. Tankards of pewter and brass and wine glasses complement the great Liverpool punch bowl decorated with scenes of the Seven Years' War.

Important New York mahogany gate-leg table, 1680–1720. Secondary woods are sycamore and tulip poplar. Length: 52 inches.

More English pottery and colorful Chinese export porcelain further reveal the kinds of wares used in this tavern. The japanned tin coffeepot on the bottom shelf is also specified in the records.

Mahogany high-post beds, as well as old leather chairs, appear in the records. The bedhangings correspond to an unusually complete entry in the estate of Henry Bowcock—"Quilt bedstead, old blue Curtains laced with yellow." Bowcock owned and ran the Raleigh Tavern in the 1720s; after his death, Wetherburn married his widow and moved in as innkeeper of the Raleigh. It is perfectly possible that Wetherburn retained such items after her death. The striped woolen blanket seen here in the east bedroom is identical to a fragment that was found preserved in the well on this site, a rare survival of a textile in the ground, compared to the millions of pieces of glass and ceramics. An easy chair of very low value (and, therefore, presumably old) was also listed in this room.

Painted blanket chest of yellow pine, made in Westmoreland County, Virginia, in the third quarter of the eighteenth century.

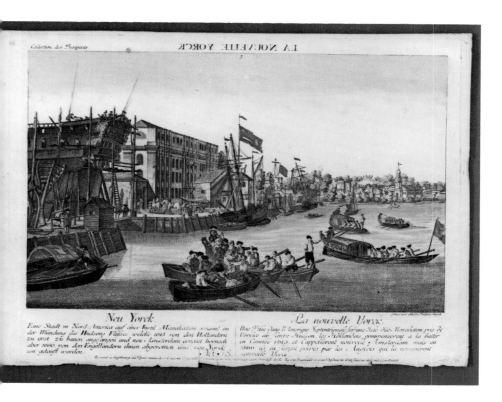

An imaginary view of New York—colored line engraving by Balthazar Frederic Leizelt of Germany about 1745; 12½ x 16¾ inches.

Bristol delft pot for the dressing table, 1740–55. Height: 3³⁄₁₆ inches. It matches fragments found on the Wetherburn property.

In contrast to the Raleigh Tavern, only nineteen beds and nine chamber pots appear in Wetherburn's inventory. The beds and coverlets seen here are common American types.

(Below)
Laundering of table, bed, and personal linen was an important part of a busy tavern. Brass irons and wooden presses were used to smooth the material out. The brass goffering iron and the standing iron in the foreground are good English examples.

American fruitwood scoop, late eighteenth century. Length: 3⅝ inches.

Even this view of the crowded, smoke-filled kitchen is not as congested as the inventory would make it seem. Almost every antique item seen here matches an entry in the inventory or fragments found in the excavations. Uncommon items specified in the former include two pairs of money scales, three spinning wheels, and thirty-two candle molds and frames.

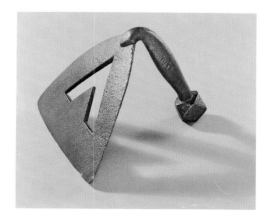

Wrought-iron scraper probably made in America at the end of the eighteenth century. Height: 3¾ inches.

Coke-Garrett House

This original building spans almost a century, from about 1750 onward. As the main central part was built in the 1830s, the house has been equipped with furnishings in the Federal or classical manner. A semi-exhibition building (the official residence of the president of the Foundation), the Coke-Garrett House expands the collections well into the first half of the nineteenth century.

Furnishings in the classical style predominate in the dining room. The table is a large Massachusetts example, the fine inlaid sideboard appears to have been made in South Carolina, and eight of the dining room chairs were made about 1793 in New York City by Robert Carter. The English silver epergne was fashioned in the early classical style by Emick Romer of London, 1775–76, while the French iron and brass chandelier was made about 1815.

Portrait of Bartholomew Dandridge, nephew of Martha Washington and private secretary to George Washington in the 1790s; painted in London about 1800 by John Trumbull. Oil on canvas, 29¾ x 25⅜ inches. It is probable that Dandridge played in Williamsburg as a boy, for his father owned a house here while judge of the General Court.

Niche table of mahogany, probably made in Baltimore, 1790–1810. Height: 34⅛ inches.

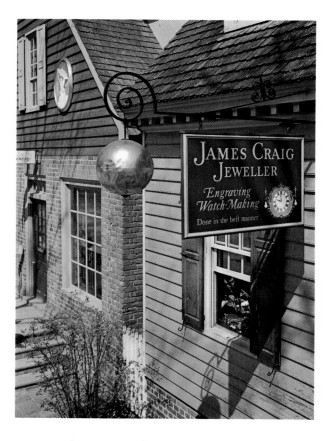

Craft Shops

For the visitor to Williamsburg the Craft Shops have one vital stimulating ingredient that the other exhibition interiors do not—people working in an eighteenth-century manner in their surroundings, so that they seem completely natural there. It is in these buildings, a number of which are shown in the following pages, that most visitors come closest to aspects of colonial life.

Clocks and a multitude of watches are exhibited at the Golden Ball, together with the items of jewelry that fashionable men and women used in profusion. The engraving of silver is practiced here now, and several cabinets contain examples of finely engraved English and American silver.

Seventeenth-century
French steel and silver
scissors case. Length: 3⅝
inches.

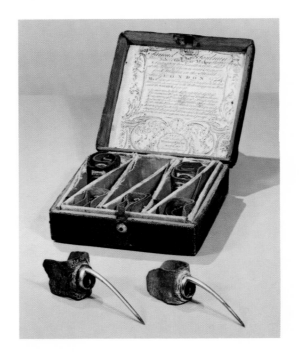

How evocative such objects can be! A set of
twelve silver cockspurs in a shagreen-covered
mahogany case, made by Samuel Toulmin in
London about 1770. On the leather attachments
to the spurs appear birds' names and numbers.
Two small paper labels give details of
cockfighting matches in the 1790s at
Newcastle-on-Tyne.

Violins, guitars, viola da gambas,
spinets, hurdy-gurdies—such
were the stringed instruments so
popular in eighteenth-century
Virginia.

Music is played and lessons are given on these instruments in the Mary Stith Shop. Seen here are eighteenth-century English instruments—an oboe, violin, bassoon, and an Aeolian harp—together with music of the kind that was popular in the colonial period.

Modern methods of exegesis, such as slide lectures, filmstrips, and movies, supplement traditional techniques—books, pamphlets, guided tours—of illustrating and explaining all phases of life in colonial Virginia. This important aspect of Colonial Williamsburg's educational program is ongoing. A still photograph from *The Music of Williamsburg* shows what was a common occurrence in eighteenth-century genteel life, a lesson on the harpsichord. It was taken in the restored mid-eighteenth century Moody House.

THE ENRAGED MUSICIAN.

William Hogarth's engraving of *The Enraged Musician,* dated 1741. Inventory and sale references prove that Hogarth's prints were immensely popular in the colonies, especially those series extolling the triumphs of virtue, industry, and honesty. They were frequently advertised for sale in eighteenth-century Williamsburg, as well as listed in inventories.

The wide variety of colorful stuffs that were available to colonial Virginians for clothes and upholstery is on display in the Margaret Hunter Shop. Accessories such as pocketbooks, small pieces of jewelry, and sewing tools were also sold here.

A woman's straw and silk hat trimmed with gauze, for summer use, made in England in the third quarter of the eighteenth century. Diameter: 14 inches.

Wood-block-printed cotton made in France in the last quarter of the eighteenth century. Width: 21½ inches.

Patch boxes, pastille boxes, necessaires, chatelaines, navettes, thimbles, needlecases, and the like, in a variety of materials ranging from mother-of-pearl to spar gypsum and tortoise shell, largely of the eighteenth century from Europe.

Delft drug pots and glass medicine bottles were the most numerous containers in the colonial apothecary shop. Fragments of such items have been frequently excavated in Williamsburg.

A walnut and yellow pine desk and bookcase from the fourth quarter of the eighteenth century, probably made in Williamsburg. It descended in the family of Dr. Galt, who owned the apothecary shop at the time the desk was made.

Few eighteenth-century wigs, of course, have survived; the two upper ones seen in the Wigmaker's Shop are original. Eighteenth-century prints of barber shops have helped in planning this exhibition interior.

The rich patina of the desk in the right foreground, the lantern, and other eighteenth-century accessories lend their colors to the tones of the new leathers that are worked at the Bootmaker's Shop in the colonial manner.

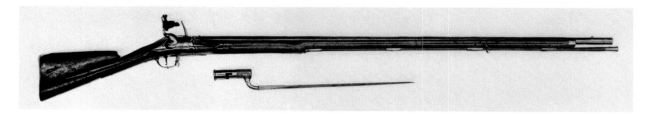

Brown Bess musket made in 1729 in England by E. Cookes. Length: 61⅛ inches.

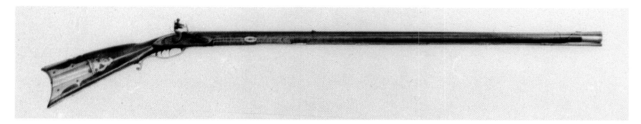

Superbly detailed long rifle, the curly maple stock mounted with engraved brass and inlaid with silver. From Pulaski County, Virginia, 1815-20, and possibly made by Abraham Honaker; 62 inches long.

The forge outside and the rifling bench inside account for two stages in the manufacture of a gun. At the left are two fine American rifles, and behind them is the patch where, over a long period of time, the gunsmith has blown the excess iron filing out of the barrel being bored.

Military paraphernalia—from pikes, pouch-boxes, and powder horns to pistols, muskets, and swords—were stored in the Magazine, which is used today to interpret the important military aspects of colonial government.

Country furniture of a simple type, prints tacked to the wall, and ordinary pottery are typical of the items one would have expected to find in the Gaol. On the table are eighteenth-century chains that were found on this site in recent times. In the corner is an unusual southern desk with a galleried top.

The Abby Aldrich Rockefeller Folk Art Collection

At the edge of the Historic Area stands the modern brick building designed for and housing the Abby Aldrich Rockefeller Folk Art Collection. With its central theme as the art of the common man and its concentration on late eighteenth- and nineteenth-century American material, the collection offers valuable and poignant insights into the society that grew out of the colonial period. Portraits and landscapes, sculpture such as weathervanes and shop signs, and utilitarian items such as pots and pans and bedcovers—where the artisan's involvement went beyond the mere function into idiosyncratic adornment—all of these present a most informative contrast to the frequently higher style objects visible in the Historic Area.

A recent exhibition of American nineteenth-century quilts and coverlets makes a colorful and exciting display on the second floor of the gallery.

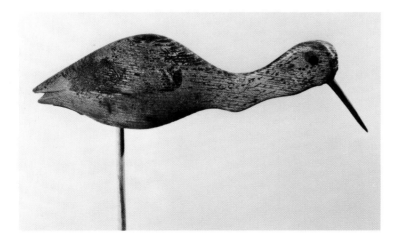

Decoy of Greater Yellowlegs carved from wood and later painted. Made probably during the nineteenth century, the piece is 11½ inches high. It was used as a lure to attract shore birds.

Ezra Weston, Jr. painted by Rufus Hathaway about 1793 in Duxbury, Massachusetts. Oil on canvas, 38 x 25 inches, in its original frame. One of a group of four portraits of this family recently acquired, all painted by the same artist. This striking portrait shows the son of the founder of a local shipping firm later described as one of the largest in America.

Polly Botsford and Her Children by an unknown artist, painted in watercolor on paper about 1815; 18¾ x 23⅞ inches. This mourning picture is an extraordinary composition in which bold, stylized forms help to create a splendid example that presages modern painting. The watercolor outlines and defines the elements, and only in the sky is it handled as a wash. The church is reduced to the elements of its framework—the idea, rather than the actual physical structure of the church. It is balanced on the left by the tree, while the center is dominated by the figures and the tombs.

Mrs. Seth Wilkinson painted in oil on wood panel by an unknown artist, about 1825–30; 30 x 23¾ inches. Several paintings can be attributed to the artist of this portrait based on the similarity of the symmetrical arrangement of the draperies and the careful painting of details, such as the jewelry and lace. It is a strong portrait—the introduction of the pet spaniel serving to bridge the distance between the sitter and the viewer.

New England painted dressing table, made of white pine, about 1835. The bold stenciled decoration makes this a vivid and attractive object. An exceptionally fine example of American painted furniture.

Birth and baptismal record of Peter Hoffman, attributed to Arnold Hoevelmann, painted in watercolor on paper in the late eighteenth century; 13 x 16 inches. An example of Pennsylvania fractur, this work gives a complete and decorative account of Hoffman's birth and baptism, including the participants, place, and time—even the sign of the zodiac.

The Talcott Family painted in watercolor on paper by Deborah Goldsmith in 1832; 14¼ x 17¾ inches. To support her aging parents, Deborah Goldsmith became a traveling artist when she was only twenty-one, in defiance of the custom that young women who wished to paint should do so only at home. *The Talcott Family* is the most ambitious of her recorded pictures, providing excellent documentation of costumes and furnishings at the time. Folk art paintings showing groups of people are rare.

Henry Ward Beecher carved from wood about 1840. Possibly by "Corbin." According to tradition, this figure (21½ x 7½ inches) represents the well-known nineteenth-century preacher, Henry Ward Beecher, and is believed to have been carved during his early pastorate in Centerville, Indiana.

The Old Plantation, late eighteen-century watercolor on paper, 11¾ x 17⅞ inches. Found in Columbia, South Carolina, it is thought that this watercolor was painted on a plantation between Charleston and Orangeburg. The paper was made in England, 1777-94, and the costumes appear to date from the last quarter of the eighteenth century. The stringed instrument is apparently a *molo*, and the drum a Yoruba instrument called *gudugudu.* The dance may well be of Yoruba origin also.

A splendid peacock of painted and decorated zinc, found in Torrington, Connecticut. It is probably an early nineteenth century tinsmith's sign; 27 inches high.

Crane, chip-carved from pine in the late nineteenth century by Aaron Mountz (1873–1949); 26½ inches high. Born in Cumberland County, Pennsylvania, Aaron Mountz was associated with Wilhelm Schimmel at an early age and carved wooden figures in a similar style.

The paneled walls of this painted room came from a house built by Alexander Shaw of Wagram, Scotland County, North Carolina, in the early nineteenth century. The painting is signed by I. Scott, although no information exists about him. He was probably an itinerant painter from the north, many of whom traveled south to Charleston executing portraits and decorating rooms in various communities en route.

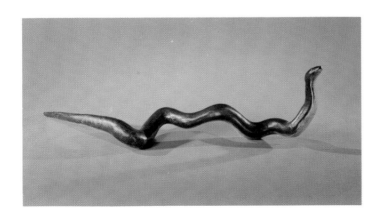

Snake, made probably in the last quarter of the eighteenth century; 18 inches long. The profile of a tree root was used to advantage in fashioning the snake, which was then made more realistic by the addition of brown and yellow paint.

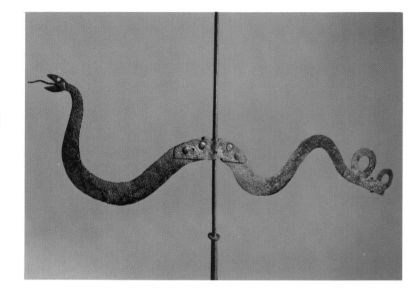

Snake weathervane, nineteenth century, made of sheet iron by an unknown artisan; 29¾ inches long.

Leedom Farm painted in oil on canvas by Edward Hicks, and dated 1849; 28 x 48 inches. The farm of David Leedom in Newtown, Bucks County, Pennsylvania, was painted by Edward Hicks in his seventieth year. The atmospheric landscape is the highest development of his art. We are fortunate in possessing an excellent group of thirteen of Hicks's paintings.

The Museum

Essentially flexible in nature, the proposed museum of decorative arts will feature not only superlative seventeenth- and eighteenth-century English and American objects from our collections, but will also house special exhibitions drawn from our own resources or from other museums. The following group of objects is among the finest at Colonial Williamsburg.

Made for William III about 1699, the superb tall-case clock of French burl walnut has works by Thomas Tompion. The ormolu mounts are of outstanding quality. Height: 115½ inches.

Made for William III in the mid 1690s by Daniel Garnier, and known to be at St. James's Palace in the eighteenth century, this chandelier is one of the monuments of English silver. Of the utmost beauty in form and decoration, it is marked only with the maker's mark, as is customary with silver destined for the royal family. Width: 33 inches.

Elaborately brocaded Spitalfields silk gown and petticoat exemplifying the rococo taste. English, 1760–70.

Monumental delft charger probably made by Christian Wilhelm at Southwark in 1648. The painted scene depicts Susanna and the Elders. Diameter: 18½ inches.

Silver-gilt two-handled covered cup of outstanding form. Made in London by the "hound sejant maker," 1649–50, it exemplifies the boldness of the best mid-seventeenth century English work. Height: 8 inches.

Hand-colored engraved map "Nova Totius Americæ Tabula," by Petrus Schenk, 1695–1705; 36 x 40 inches. It appears to be the only known impression of this handsome Dutch map.

[115]

Two charming versions of the Chinaman teapot, made at Chelsea, 1745–49. Height: 6¾ inches.

Magnificent silver tureen fashioned by George Wickes in advanced rococo taste for Thomas Watson, earl of Malton and later first marquess of Rockingham. The griffin handles are derived from the coat of arms, which is also cast and applied to each side. 1737–38, London. Weight: 171 ounces.

The only recorded pair of Wrotham candlesticks, made of slip-decorated earthenware and dated 1668. Height: 10⅞ inches. Strongly modeled and boldly colored, the candlesticks are attributed to George Richardson.

Splendid tablecover of linen and cotton decorated with wool embroidery, 1650–75; 38 x 48 inches.

The only known piece of English pewter with an engraved portrait of James II, this is one of the finest of late Stuart tankards. It was made in London by John Donne about 1685. Height: 7½ inches.

One of an original set of twelve mahogany open arm chairs, 1750–60, from Glenham, Suffolk, seat of Lord North. According to family tradition, the needlework upholstery designs were drawn and worked by Lady Barbara North.

Pewter two-handled covered porringer by John Langford, Sr., of London, about 1720. Length: 10 1/16 inches. Commemorating the Treaty of Ryswick of 1697, the porringer was probably cast from existing molds in 1722 on the occasion of the death of John Churchill, the duke of Marlborough. Only a score of English pewter commemorative porringers are known. The relief cast decoration is of the finest quality.

A silver sugar box made in Boston, Massachusetts, by John Coney, 1690–1710, in an elaborate and rare American baroque form. Length: 7¼ inches.

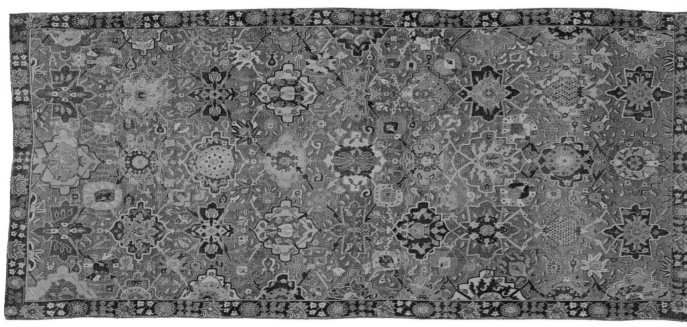

"Vase carpet" from Kerman, southwest Persia, made in the second half of the seventeenth century.

Newport, Rhode Island, tall-case clock with the works by William Claggett, 1745–60. The rich color contrasts of mahogany, silver, brass, and the red wool behind the pierced and engraved brass fret (restored on the evidence of an original fragment) accentuate the boldly modeled forms of this commanding piece. Height: 100¼ inches.

One of a pair of rare pewter tureens by Thomas Chamberlain of London, about 1750. Length: 15½ inches. Engraved with the arms of Richard Edgcumbe of Mount Edgcumbe, Devon.

In this modern storage area our superb collection of textiles is kept free from dust and light. Textiles in the exhibition buildings are constantly changed.

One of a pair of silver-gilt fruit baskets and stands with their original cut-glass basins made in London by Wakelin and Taylor, 1787–90, for the second duke of Newcastle. They are superb examples of the Adam style fashioned in English silver, with the most exquisite detail, and are fully recorded in the silversmiths' account books.

A magnificent Charleston easy chair of the last quarter of the eighteenth century made of mahogany, American southern cypress, and yellow pine. Height: 45⅜ inches. By tradition, the chair belonged to the family of Governor Robert Daniel of Charleston, South Carolina. The needlework upholstery is of the period.

Storage is essential for objects being prepared for exhibition. A shed is planned to be built by Colonial Williamsburg craftsmen on Market Square Green for the eighteenth-century fire engine seen here. There is a record of such a machine in that location in the colonial period. Prints are rotated frequently so that they are not over-exposed to light. The clock and the set of chairs on the rack are being held in readiness for possible installation at Carter's Grove.

[120]

DEPARTMENT OF COLLECTIONS

Graham S. Hood, *Director of Collections and Vice-President of the Colonial Williamsburg Foundation*

Curatorial Staff of the Department of Collections

John C. Austin, *Curator of Ceramics and Glass*
John D. Davis, *Curator of Metalwork*
Mrs. Joan D. Dolmetsch, *Curator of Prints and Maps*
Barry A. Greenlaw, *Curator of Furniture*
Wallace B. Gusler, *Curator of Mechanical Arts*
Miss Mildred B. Lanier, *Curator of Textiles*
Miss Sandra C. Shaffer, *Assistant Curator*

Mrs. Eleanor Duncan, now interior design consultant for the Division of Visitor Accommodations, rendered invaluable service as associate curator to John Graham for twelve years, before her 1970 retirement.

CONSERVATION STAFF

Robert F. Simms, *Conservator of Furniture*
P. Richard Simms, *Apprentice Cabinetmaker*
Mrs. Violet M. Simms, *Conservator*
Paul I. Garnett, *Preparator*
Leroy O. Graves, *Preparator*

OFFICE STAFF

Mrs. Janet L. Smith, *Administrative Assistant*
Mrs. Margaret S. Gill, *Research Archivist*
Miss Susan K. Gibson, *Librarian*
Mrs. Dorothy B. Wing, *Registrar*
Mrs. Donna M. Wilson, *Assistant Registrar*
Mrs. Frances Davis, *Secretary*
Mrs. Janice L. Oakes, *Secretary*

PHOTOGRAPHERS

Delmore A. Wenzel
Hans E. Lorenz

Curatorial Staff of the Abby Aldrich Rockefeller Folk Art Collection

Miss Beatrix T. Rumford, *Associate Director*
Donald R. Walters, *Assistant Curator*
Miss Barbara R. Luck, *Registrar*
Mrs. Kathleen F. Vermillion, *Assistant Registrar*
Mrs. Carrie S. Galloway, *Administrative Assistant*

CUSTODIANS—PREPARATORS

Douglas Canady
Osborne Taylor

DOCENTS

Mrs. Lucy Gunn
Mrs. Helen Mahone
Mrs. Anne Warlow

THE WILLIAMSBURG COLLECTION OF ANTIQUE FURNISHINGS
was composed by Typographic Service Incorporated, Philadelphia, Pennsylvania in
Intertype (Fototronic) Elegante, and lithographed by W. M. Brown and Son, Richmond,
Virginia. The binding for the paperbound edition was done by the William Byrd Press,
Richmond, Virginia, and that for the clothbound edition by Haddon Craftsmen, Scran-
ton, Pennsylvania. The paper is Oxford's Starflex. N. Jane Iseley did the scene photo-
graphy, Delmore A. Wenzel and Hans E. Lorenz did the museum photography, and
Richard J. Stinely designed the book; all are members of the Colonial Williamsburg staff.